LEVEL **2** SCIENCE
LET'S READ AND **FIND OUT**

GERMS MAKE ME SICK!

BY MELVIN BERGER

ILLUSTRATED BY MARYLIN HAFNER

He's sick!

HARPER
An Imprint of HarperCollinsPublishers

The paintings for this book were done in pen and ink and watercolor on Arches watercolor paper.
With special thanks to Melanie Marin, M.D., for her expert advice.

The Let's-Read-and-Find-Out Science book series was originated by Dr. Franklyn M. Branley, Astronomer Emeritus and former Chairman of the American Museum of Natural History–Hayden Planetarium, and was formerly co-edited by him and Dr. Roma Gans, Professor Emeritus of Childhood Education, Teachers College, Columbia University. Text and illustrations for each of the books in the series are checked for accuracy by an expert in the relevant field. For more information about Let's-Read-and-Find-Out Science books, write to HarperCollins Children's Books, 195 Broadway, New York, NY 10007, or visit our website at www.letsreadandfindout.com.

Let's Read-and-Find-Out Science® is a trademark of HarperCollins Publishers.

Library of Congress Cataloging-in-Publication Data
Berger, Melvin.
   Germs make me sick! / by Melvin Berger ; illustrated by Marylin Hafner.
— Rev. ed.
      p.   cm. — (Let's-read-and-find-out science. Stage 2)
   Summary: Explains how bacteria and viruses affect the human body and how the body fights them.
   ISBN 978-0-06-238187-3
   1. Bacteria—Juvenile literature.   2. Viruses—Juvenile literature.   3. Bacterial diseases—Juvenile literature.   4. Virus diseases—Juvenile literature.   [1. Bacteria. 2. Viruses.]   I. Hafner, Marylin, ill.   II. Title.   III. Series.
QR57.B47   1995   93-27059
616.9'2—dc20   CIP
                                                                                        AC

16 17 18 19   SCP   10 9 8 7 6 5 4

❖

Revised edition, 2015

GERMS
MAKE ME SICK!

You wake up one morning. But you don't feel like getting out of bed. Your arms and legs ache. Your head hurts. You have a fever. And your throat is sore.

"I'm sick," you say. "I must have caught a germ."

Everyone knows that germs can make you sick. But not everyone knows how.

5

Germs are tiny living things. They are far too small to see with your eyes alone. In fact, a line of one thousand germs could fit across the top of a pencil!

There are many different kinds of germs. But the two that usually make you sick are bacteria and viruses.

Under a microscope, some bacteria look like little round balls. Others are as straight as rods. Still others are twisted in spiral shapes.

 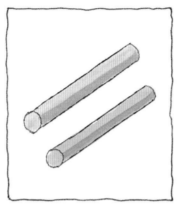 

Viruses are far tinier than bacteria. Some look like balls with spikes sticking out on all sides. Others look like loaves of bread or like tadpoles. There are even some that look like metal screws with spider legs.

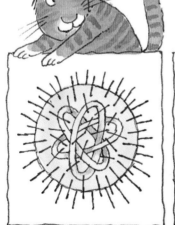 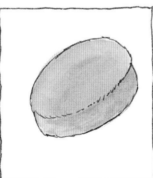  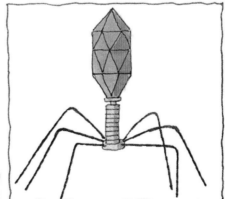

Germs, such as bacteria and viruses, are found everywhere. They are in the air you breathe, in the food you eat, in the water you drink, and on everything you touch. They are even on your skin and in your body.

Although germs are all around, they do not always make you sick. Many germs are not harmful. Also, your body keeps out harmful germs most of the time.

Your skin blocks the germs. As long as there are no cuts or scratches on your skin, germs can't get in.

Your nose helps, too. It is lined with tiny hairs.
The hairs catch many of the germs you breathe in.
They push them back out.

The inside of your mouth and throat is always wet. Germs
often get stuck there. They don't go any farther.

Yet some germs do slip in every once in a while.

Your friend has a cold. She sneezes. Germs fly out. You breathe the air. Some of her germs may get into your lungs.

You take a sip of your cousin's soda. Her germs are on the straw. A few of the germs may get into your stomach.

You're riding a bike. You fall and scrape your knee. Germs from the ground may get under your skin.

But even when harmful bacteria and viruses get into your body, you don't always get sick. That is because your body has ways to fight germs.

That will have to be cleaned thoroughly.

The white cells in your blood go after any germs that sneak in. Usually, these cells kill the germs before they can do any harm.

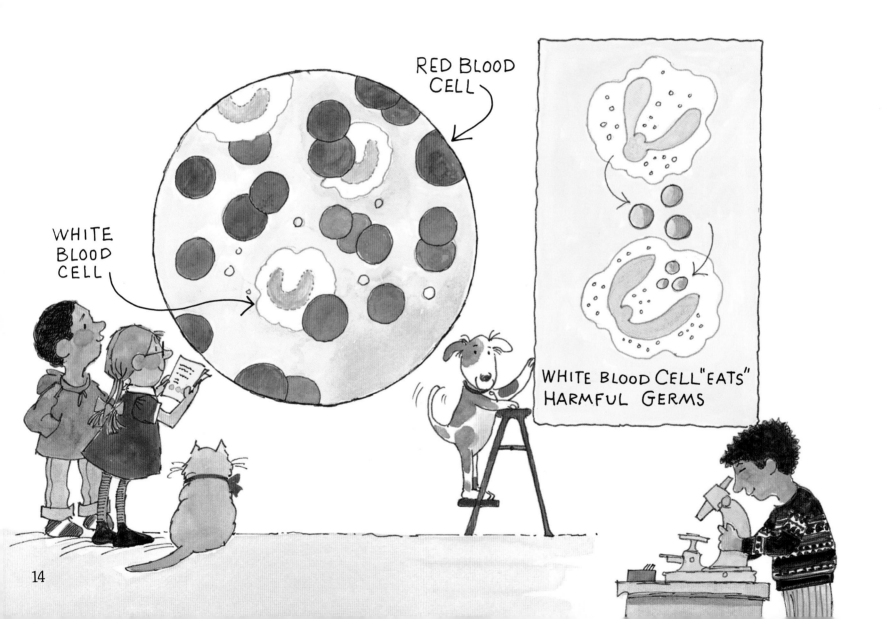

RED BLOOD CELL

WHITE BLOOD CELL

WHITE BLOOD CELL "EATS" HARMFUL GERMS

Your blood also has special proteins that attack germs.
They are called antibodies.

The white blood cells and antibodies don't always get rid of
the germs, though. Some germs stay in the body and make
you sick.

What if the germs in your body are bacteria? They quickly start to multiply. Each one becomes two new bacteria. Then they become four, and so on. In a few hours there may be millions of bacteria in your body.

The bacteria give off waste products. Some of these wastes
are poisons. The poisons can damage or kill the cells that
make up your body. When enough cells are harmed, you feel
sick.

You may have pains and aches, run a fever, or break out in a rash. You may cough or sneeze or throw up. These signs tell you that cells are being damaged or killed in your body.

Some bacteria give off poisons that stay close to the bacteria. Bacteria in your mouth are like that. Their poison attacks only your teeth and causes cavities. It does not go to other places in your body.

Earaches and boils on the skin can also be caused by bacteria whose poisons stay in one place.

Other bacteria give off poisons that move around the body. One kind of bacteria lives in the lungs. But it gives off poisons that are carried around in the blood. These bacteria may give you a headache or a sore stomach.

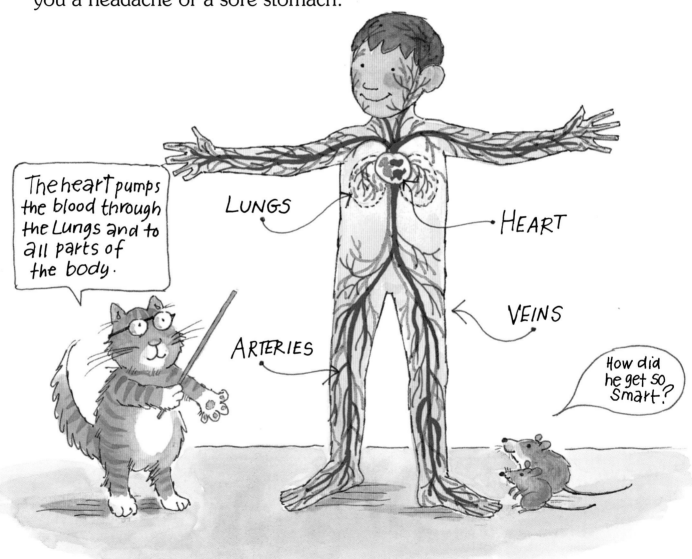

Still other bacteria have poisons in their outer coats. When they touch different cells, their poisons hurt or destroy them. As the cells die, you feel sick.

What if viruses get into your body? Viruses are different from bacteria. They don't give off poisons. Each virus forces its way into a body cell. It disappears inside. For a while, nothing seems to be happening. Then, suddenly, the viruses break out of the cell. Hundreds of new viruses tumble out.

Each virus finds another cell and digs its way in. Then these cells pop open, and more viruses pour out. Soon there are millions of viruses in your body.

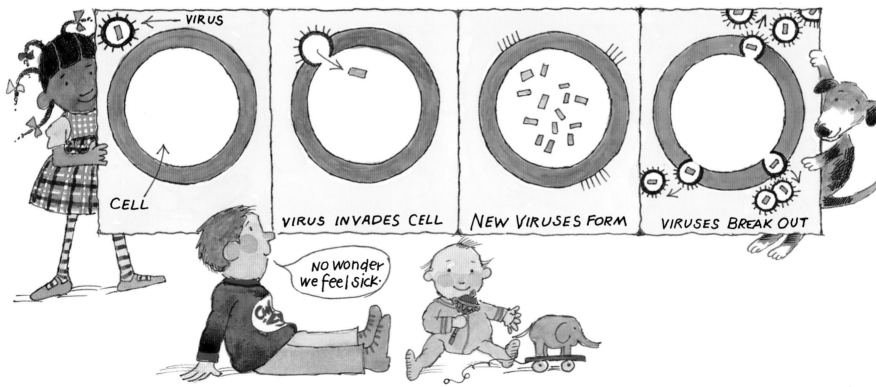

VIRUS

CELL

VIRUS INVADES CELL

NEW VIRUSES FORM

VIRUSES BREAK OUT

No wonder we feel sick.

The viruses spread out. As they do, you feel worse and worse. Viruses bring you colds and the flu, measles, mumps, and chicken pox, and lots of other illnesses.

Though bacteria and viruses can make you sick, you usually begin to feel better after a day or two. Your body has beaten back the germs.

At times, though, you feel very sick. Or you stay sick for days. Then you should see a doctor. Doctors try to find out which germs are making you sick.

"What hurts?" they ask. "Let's take a look."

Perhaps they swab your throat with cotton. Then they send
the cotton with the germs on it to a lab. Or they may take a
few drops of blood from your fingertip or arm. That also goes
to a lab to be tested.

Your doctor gets a report from the lab. It tells whether the germs are bacteria or viruses. If bacteria are making you sick, the doctor usually prescribes some drug. The drug will either kill the bacteria or stop them from growing.

Doctors do not yet have drugs to cure diseases caused by viruses. But they can give you shots to prevent some of these diseases.

If you do get sick with a virus, the doctor may give you some medicine anyway. It won't cure you, but it might help you feel better, or protect you against bacteria that might make you even sicker.

When germs make you sick, your doctor might tell you to stay in bed. Bed rest makes it easier for your body to fight the germs. So do eating and drinking healthy foods and drinks.

Once you are well, you want to stay that way. There are lots of ways to keep healthy.

31

Germs do make you sick—sometimes. But you can help
yourself be as fit as a fiddle all the rest of the time!